# UKRAINE

BY A. R. CARSER

An Imprint of Abdo Publishing
abdobooks.com

**ABDOBOOKS.COM**

Published by Abdo Publishing, a division of ABDO, PO Box 398166, Minneapolis, Minnesota 55439. 

Printed in the United States of America, North Mankato, Minnesota.
102022
012023

Cover Photos: Leonid Andronov/Shutterstock (Pechersk Lavra); Sofiia Sysa/Shutterstock (pattern)
Interior Photos: Ruslan Lytvyn/Shutterstock, 4–5; Shutterstock, 6, 10, 24, 26, 37, 39, 63, 70–71, 74, 76–77, 90–91; UBC Stock/Shutterstock, 9; Zysko Sergii/Shutterstock, 11; Andrey Nekrasov/Image Broker/Getty Images, 12–13; Anton Starikov/Shutterstock, 14; Peter Hermes Furian/Shutterstock, 15 (Ukraine); Web Tools/Shutterstock, 15 (globe); Jay Si/Shutterstock, 16; Anton Petrus/Moment/Getty Images, 17; Sergej Onyshko/Shutterstock, 18; Goinyk Production/Shutterstock, 20; Rudmer Zwerver/Shutterstock, 22–23; Kotenko Oleksandr/Shutterstock, 29; Rubén Chase Carbó/Moment/Getty Images, 31; Diego Grandi/Shutterstock, 32–33; Tara Walton/Toronto Star/Getty Images, 34; Fine Art Images/Heritage Images/Hulton Archive/Getty Images, 36; Fine Art Images/Heritage Images/Hulton Fine Art Collection/Getty Images, 41; Everett Collection/Shutterstock, 43; Buyenlarge/Archive Photos/Getty Images, 45; Sergii Kharchenko/Pacific Press/Light Rocket/Getty Images, 47; SHONE/Gamma-Rapho/Getty Images, 49; Sergii Kharchenko/NurPhoto/Getty Images, 50; Andrei Mosienko/AFP/Getty Images, 52; Louisa Gouliamaki/AFP/Getty Images, 54; Marco Bertorello/AFP/Getty Images, 56–57; Ivan Popovych/Shutterstock, 59; Dominika Zarzycka/NurPhoto/Getty Images, 61; Culture Club/Hulton Archive/Getty Images, 65; Serhii Hudak/Ukrinform/Future Publishing/Getty Images, 66; Lipatova Maryna/Shutterstock, 68; Janek Skarzynski/AFP/Getty Images, 72; Ukrinform/Future Publishing/Getty Images, 75; Yurii Borysov/Shutterstock, 79; Maxym Marusenko/NurPhoto/Getty Images, 80–81; Volodymyr Maksymchuk/Shutterstock, 82; Daniil Petrov/Shutterstock, 84; Andriy Solovyov/Shutterstock, 85; Ruslan Harutyunov/Shutterstock, 87; Oleksandr Gimanov/AFP/Getty Images, 93; Alexey Nikolsky/Sputnik/AFP/Getty Images, 94; Chris McGrath/Getty Images News/Getty Images, 99; Kamil Adgozalli/Shutterstock, 101

Editor: Priscilla An
Series Designer: Maggie Villaume

Library of Congress Control Number: 2022940386

**PUBLISHER'S CATALOGING-IN-PUBLICATION DATA**

Names: Carser, A. R., author.
Title: Ukraine / by A. R. Carser
Description: Minneapolis, Minnesota: Abdo Publishing, 2023 | Series: Essential Library of Countries | Includes online resources and index.
Identifiers: ISBN 9781532199493 (lib. bdg.) | ISBN 9781098274696 (ebook)
Subjects: LCSH: Ukraine--Juvenile literature. | Europe--Juvenile literature. | Ukraine--History--Juvenile literature. | Geography--Juvenile literature.
Classification: DDC 947.7--dc23

# CONTENTS

CHAPTER **ONE**

# MEMORIES OF UKRAINE

Whenever her nieces come to visit, Akanni and the girls make *golubtsi*, or Ukrainian cabbage rolls. Making the dish is a labor of love. It reminds Akanni of her time at the Dnipro State Medical University in Dnipro, Ukraine. Today, Akanni is a doctor in Lagos, Nigeria, her hometown. But several years ago, she was a medical student in Ukraine. She was one of a dozen African students in her program.

**In 2021, Dnipro had a population of 51,821 people.**[1]

Kyiv, Ukraine's capital, is a city with a rich cultural history.

**People in western Ukraine make small golubtsi rolls with the cabbage leaf divided into two pieces.**

Akanni makes the cabbage roll stuffing ahead of time. The savory aroma of pork, beef, and carrots fills her kitchen. Instead of white rice, she mixes in jollof rice to add a touch of Nigerian cuisine. Once they arrive, Akanni's nieces stuff cabbage leaves with the mixture. They place the leaves in the bottom of Akanni's cast-iron pot. When the girls are done, Akanni covers the cabbage rolls with *podliva*. Podliva is a sauce made from carrots, sour cream, mushrooms, and marinara sauce. Together, Akanni and her nieces wait as the rolls simmer on the stove. Then they pop the rolls into the oven. After hours of prep and cooking time, the golubtsi are finally ready to enjoy.

Akanni's first bite takes her back to the small kitchen in her apartment in Dnipro. Dnipro is a city in east-central Ukraine. Her Ukrainian roommate, Kalyna, made golubtsi once a month as a treat. The delicious smell would

## FOREIGN STUDENTS IN UKRAINE

In 2020, about 80,000 people studied abroad in Ukraine. They represented 158 countries.[3] More than 20,000 Indian students studied at Ukraine's universities. So did nearly 16,000 students from Nigeria, Morocco, and Egypt.[4] For many students, universities in Ukraine were more affordable than schools in the United States or Europe. Students earned degrees in science, technology, medicine, and engineering.

fill their apartment. Sometimes, Kalyna would offer leftovers to their elderly neighbors. When the weather was nice, Kalyna and Akanni would walk along Dnipro Quay. They never walked the entire way, since the quay was 14 miles (23 km) long.[2] Sometimes, they would stop at White Swan Fountain and grab a coffee from one of the cafés that line the quay. Once, when the weather was bad, Akanni spent the day at the National Historical Museum. There, she learned all about Ukraine's prehistoric civilizations and its more recent history as a former member of the Soviet Union.

On some weekends, Akanni and Kalyna took trips across the country. Once, they visited Kyiv, Ukraine's capital. They explored Maidan Nezalezhnosti, the city center, and walked along Khreshchatyk, the city's main street. After people-watching in the square, Akanni and Kalyna spent a couple of hours shopping in the underground market under Maidan Nezalezhnosti. Then they walked south out of the square along Khreshchatyk. They smiled at the people dressed in their finest who were also out for a stroll. When they got hungry, they popped into one of the little cafés for a treat. The next day, Akanni and Kalyna donned skirts and head coverings and spent the morning at Kyiv-Pechersk Lavra. The World Heritage site is a complex of Eastern Orthodox churches and bell towers. Akanni marveled at the human-made caves under Kyiv-Pechersk Lavra that dated back to the 1000s CE.

One summer, Akanni and Kalyna took a trip south to Odesa. Odesa is a city on Ukraine's Black Sea coast. They took in the sunshine, food, and shops near the Arcadia and Lanzheron Beaches. They got tired climbing up and down the 192 steps of the Potemkin Stairs that connected the city to the port. Exhausted, they ate lunch outside at one of the restaurants on Vul Derybasivska, Odesa's main street.

Akanni enjoyed her visits to Ukraine's cities. But her favorite trip was to the Carpathian Mountains in southwestern Ukraine. She and Kalyna joined other medical students for a week of hiking and sightseeing. The mountains were about a 14-hour drive from Dnipro. The group flew to Lviv in western Ukraine and drove south to Synevyr National Nature Park. There, Akanni and her friends hiked around Lake Synevyr, Ukraine's largest and deepest mountain lake. On a trip to one of the park's many waterfalls, the group spotted a brown bear and a golden eagle. The photos Akanni took on that trip decorated her apartment in Lagos.

### UKRAINE'S CHURCHES

Ukraine is a religious country, with most of its citizens identifying as Eastern Orthodox, a type of Christianity. Hundreds of churches can be found across the country. During Soviet rule in the 1900s, many of these churches were destroyed because their influence threatened the Soviet government's power. However, several historical churches survived, including Kyiv's Pechersk Lavra monastery. The Cathedral of Saint Sophia in Kyiv is the country's oldest church. It was built in 1017 CE. Its mosaics and frescoes impress visitors and worshippers alike.

**Lake Synevyr is located within the Carpathian Mountains. The picturesque lake is one of Ukraine's natural wonders.**

After her nieces left, Akanni sat down and glanced at her phone. She was shocked to see several notifications about Ukraine. She knew Russian forces had been gathering along Ukraine's northern border with Belarus. However, like her Ukrainian friends, Akanni did not think Russia would actually invade Ukraine. It seemed that she and her friends were wrong. Worried, Akanni texted Kalyna and her other friends still living in Ukraine. She wanted to make sure they were safe.

## BUILDING A NATION

Despite political uncertainty, Ukrainians have worked to build a shared cultural identity. More than 77 percent of the people who live in the country identify as Ukrainian, while more than 17 percent identify as Russian.[5] Ukraine is home to Eastern Europeans as well as a growing number of people from Nigeria and other African nations who study and work there. People from India, Morocco, and Egypt also study in Ukraine.

Ukrainians work a variety of jobs. Much of the land is ideal for farming. Many farmers grow food and other agricultural products. Other people work in the iron industry or build military weapons or other equipment. However, most work some sort of service job.

Ukrainians enjoy several pastimes. Soccer is extremely popular. Many people cheer on the Ukraine National Football Teams. Others visit the theaters, opera companies, and ballet companies in the country's cities. Museums and galleries are also popular ways to spend free time. From golubtsi and underground markets to soccer and opera, Ukraine is a country with a rich national identity.

## UKRAINE NATIONAL FOOTBALL TEAMS

Ukrainians love to cheer on their national soccer teams. In 2022, the Ukraine National Football Team ranked twenty-seventh out of 211 teams in the men's division of FIFA, the international governing organization for soccer.[6] That year, the men's national soccer team was just one win away from competing at the World Cup.

Ukrainians display their patriotism on the Independence Day of Ukraine. This holiday is celebrated on August 24.

CHAPTER **TWO**

# GEOGRAPHY

Ukraine is Europe's largest country after Russia, spanning 233,032 square miles (603,550 sq km).[1] It is 785 miles (1,263 km) wide and 346 miles (557 km) from north to south.[2] Located in southeast Europe, Ukraine lies east of Poland and Slovakia, south of Belarus, west of Russia, and north of the Black Sea and the Sea of Azov.

With the exception of the Carpathian Mountains in the southwest, Ukraine's land is steppe. Steppe is a vast plains region that is flat and mostly treeless. It covers 95 percent of the country's area.[3] Ukraine's steppe contains highlands that stretch from the northwest corner of the country to its southeastern frontier. In the north, these highlands are forested steppe, where

Most of Ukraine's land is steppe, which is a dry, grassy plain without any trees or tall plants.

trees dot the plains landscape. However, few trees are found naturally in the southern highlands and lowlands.

Ukraine's steppe has long been the country's most important natural resource. Two-thirds of the country contains an especially fertile black soil called chernozem. It is found in central and southern Ukraine. Chernozem contains nutrients that are ideal for crops. Ukrainian agricultural products feed people in the Middle East, North Africa, and China.

The Dnipro River cuts through Ukraine from north to south. In the north, the river flows through the Pripet Marshes. Parts of these marshlands are within the Polissia Nature Reserve. The Dnipro River empties into the Black Sea in the south. Several large reservoirs create long, skinny lakes along the Dnipro River. The largest is the Kremenchuk Reservoir in central Ukraine. It was formed in 1954 after the Kremenchuk hydroelectric dam was completed. Other notable rivers in Ukraine include the Buh and Dnister Rivers in the west and

## WHY IS UKRAINE'S SOIL SO FERTILE?

Ukraine's chernozem black soil is one of the most fertile soils in the entire world. It is rich in humus, nutrient-rich organic matter that is created by decomposing plants and animals. Ukraine's most fertile steppe contains approximately five feet (1.5 m) of humus below the grassland's surface.[4] Animal activity within the soil also makes it ideal for growing crops. Burrowing animals, such as earthworms, mice, and squirrels, dig in the soil to avoid temperature extremes in the winter and summer months. This mixes the soil layers and creates an ideal place for plants to take root.

# MAP OF UKRAINE

**KEY:**

- Capital
- City
- Point of Interest

The Dnipro River is the fourth-longest river in Europe. It passes through major cities, including Kyiv and Dnipro.

**The Carpathian Mountains stretch across the borders of seven different countries: the Czech Republic, Serbia, Slovakia, Poland, Hungary, Ukraine, and Romania.**

the Donets River in the east. These rivers all flow south into the Black Sea or the Sea of Azov. The Danube River, which begins in southwest Germany, flows into the Black Sea in Ukraine's southwesternmost point.

## EXTREME GEOGRAPHY

While most of Ukraine is flat, fertile steppe, there are a few places of extreme geography. The Carpathian Mountains span the southwest region of Ukraine. They contain Mount Hoverla, the highest point in Ukraine. The Carpathian range, as well as the area north and west of the mountains, contains

**Ukraine's highest peak is Mount Hoverla, which is 6,762 feet (2,061 m) tall.[5]**

**Oleshky Sands is a semiarid desert. It is one of the biggest sandy areas in Europe.**

pine forest. Several rivers and tributaries, including the Dnister River, originate in the Carpathian Mountains, swelling with snowmelt in the spring as they flow to the Black Sea.

Part of the Carpathian Mountains is protected by the Carpathian National Nature Park, Ukraine's first and largest national park. It has landmarks such as Mount Hoverla and Nesamovyte Lake. The park is home to approximately 48 mammal species, including the brown bear, wolf, and Eurasian otter.

The extreme southwestern corner of Ukraine is home to Europe's largest wetland, covering 2,239 square miles (5,800 sq km).[6] It is formed within the Danube River's delta, the marshland where the river joins the Black Sea. The wetland is an important habitat for many waterbirds, such as pelicans, herons, and storks.

Far from the wetlands of the Danube delta is the Oleshky Sands National Nature Park.

## KARADAG NATURE RESERVE

The Karadag Nature Reserve is located on the Crimean Peninsula. It contains the only mountain formation in Europe that dates from the Jurassic period. The range was formed by prehistoric activity of the Karadag volcano. The unique landscape within the Karadag Nature Reserve is home to rock formations created by lava flows, valuable minerals, and thousands of plant and animal species.

The Oleshky Sands are a natural desert in southern Ukraine, southeast of the city of Kherson. The rolling sand dunes cover 618 square miles (1,600 sq km).[7] Trails crisscross the desert. They are popular with ATV and dune buggy riders. To stop the spread of the desert into the surrounding landscape, the Ukrainian government planted forests around the desert. Scientists study the desert at a research station within the park.

## COASTAL UKRAINE

Ukraine's southern coast along the Black Sea and Sea of Azov is its third major landscape. It includes the Black Sea lowlands in the west, the Azov highlands in the east, and the Crimean Peninsula. The Black Sea lowlands slope gently toward the coast. Where the Azov highlands meet the Sea of Azov, long, narrow spits of sandy land jut out into the water. The longest is the Arabat Spit, which extends 70 miles (113 km) into the Sea of Azov. However, it averages less than five miles (8 km) wide.[8]

The Isthmus of Perekop connects the Crimean Peninsula to the rest of Ukraine. The Crimean Peninsula separates the Black Sea from the Sea of Azov. It contains lowland steppe as well as a range of mountains to the south of the peninsula called the Crimean Mountains. The highest point

**In the winter months, some Ukrainians and travelers go to Bukovel, a popular ski resort located in the Ukrainian Carpathian Mountains.**

in the range is Mount Roman-Kosh. It stands 5,069 feet (1,545 m) tall.[9] However, about 75 percent of the Crimean Peninsula is steppe.[10] The southern coast of the peninsula is warm in the summer, with mild, rainy winters. It is a popular place for Ukrainians to vacation in the warmer months.

## UKRAINE'S CLIMATE

Ukraine's climate is temperate, though different regions experience different climate conditions. Eastern Ukraine experiences greater temperature swings than western Ukraine does.

In northeastern Ukraine, for example, the average January temperature is 18 degrees Fahrenheit (–8°C). The average July temperature in southeastern Ukraine is 73 degrees Fahrenheit (23°C).[11]

Temperatures in western Ukraine are more moderate. For example, the average January temperature in the southwest is 26 degrees Fahrenheit (–3°C). The average July temperature in the northwest is 64 degrees Fahrenheit (18°C).[12] Western Ukraine typically receives more precipitation each year than eastern and southeastern Ukraine.

Along the southern coast of the Crimean Peninsula, residents and vacationers enjoy a climate similar to that along the Mediterranean coast, such as in Nice, France, and Athens, Greece. There, dry and hot summers give way to mild, rainy winters. Snow rarely falls along Crimea's southern coast.

### ENVIRONMENTAL CONCERNS IN UKRAINE

Decades of heavy industry and intensive farming have created several environmental concerns in Ukraine. Air pollution from coal-burning industries is severe in eastern Ukraine, especially in the cities. In central and western Ukraine, rivers are polluted with fertilizer runoff from surrounding farms. Untreated sewage also pollutes rivers. In June 2021, scientists detected more than 160 chemicals and metals in the Dnipro River.[13] Government officials have promised to pass laws to limit chemicals in detergents and single-use plastics. However, these measures will not clean up the chemicals already present in the water. Experts recommend that Ukraine upgrade its aging wastewater systems to clean up the nation's rivers.

CHAPTER **THREE**

# PLANTS AND ANIMALS

Much of Ukraine's land is cultivated, or developed for agriculture. Despite this, the country has many wild landscapes, including several national nature preserves. Many plants and animals live in Ukraine's steppe, forests, mountains, and rivers, as well as along its coast.

The forest-steppe in north-central Ukraine contains mixed woodland tree species, including oak, elm, maple, pine, and willow. Tree cover gradually thins toward the south. The steppe of southern Ukraine is flat and treeless. While most of this land is cultivated, nature preserves protect natural prairie grasses such as fescue and feather grasses. Fescues are short, clumpy

The great bustard is one of the heaviest flying birds, weighing up to 31 pounds (14 kg). The bird lives in the steppes of Ukraine and in grasslands throughout Europe.

**The European hamster was added to the critically endangered animals list in 2020.**

grasses, while feather grasses are long, with feathery tops. Meadow sage, with long, purple flowers, also grows there, along with steppe tulips and almond shrubs.

Most of the southern steppe's mammals are rodents. Rabbits, marmots, hamsters, mice, and European mole rats make burrows in the steppe's soil. These prey animals attract predators such as foxes, wolves, and polecats. Larks, quail, partridges, and yellow buntings are common bird species in the Ukrainian steppe. Larger raptors such as owls and eagles also live in the steppe. Additionally, the steppe is home to Europe's heaviest flying bird, the great bustard. Adult male bustards are noticeable with their bulging necks, heavy bodies, and chestnut back feathers streaked with black. The animals of the forest-steppe include a mix of these steppe species as well as forest animals such as bobcats, woodpeckers, and squirrels.

Due to the intensive land use from agriculture and land development, populations of native plant and animal species have dwindled in the grassland habitat. The Podolsk blind mole rat is one example. It is a vulnerable species of rodent native to the Ukrainian steppe. Other small endangered species such as the European hamster also live in the steppe.

### ASKANIYA-NOVA, UKRAINE'S FIRST NATURE PRESERVE

Covering an area of 127 square miles (330 sq km) in southern Ukraine, Askaniya-Nova Nature Reserve is surrounded by farmland.[2] The oldest steppe reserve in the world, it was created in 1888 as a preserve for plants and a breeding center for threatened species. Now the park is an oasis for many of the plants and animals native to the Ukrainian steppe. Several species of feather grass carpet the area, as do wild tulips and other flowering plants. More than 250 bird species migrate through the park each year. The park is home to 480 protected animal species.[3]

Ukraine has worked to protect its native plants and animals. Nature preserves in the steppe help sustain threatened species. These protected areas allow native plants and animals to survive. At the Askaniya-Nova Nature Reserve in southern Ukraine, breeding programs have increased the numbers of onagers and Przewalski's horses. These are wild species in the horse family.

## PLANTS AND ANIMALS OF THE POLISSIA

One-quarter of the land of the Polissia woodland and marshland in northern Ukraine is covered with forest. Pine trees make up 60 percent of the tree species in these forests.[1] Oak, birch, and aspen trees

Polissia is a historic region covered with forests and swamps.

also grow in the Polissia woodland. The marshlands of Polissia are home to mosses, sedges, willow trees, and birch trees.

Because of its varying habitats, Polissia is home to more diverse animal species than the forest-steppe and steppe. Eurasian red squirrels, brown bears, and forest martens, members of the weasel family, all live in Ukraine's northern forests and marshlands. Though rare, elk sometimes visit the marshy forest to graze. The marshlands are home to beavers, European otters, and mink. Many waterfowl species live in the marshlands too, including ducks, gulls, and kingfishers. Several species of fish in the carp family, as well as pike and perch, swim in the waters of northern Ukraine.

Overhunting and loss of habitat reduced the animal population in the Polissia region. Some species, such as elk and bears, have migrated north to seek stabler habitats. Others have been hunted nearly to extinction. The European bison used to roam the forest and forest-steppe of Ukraine. Decades of overhunting and warfare reduced the European bison population to just 48 after World War I (1914–1918). In the 1960s, surviving animals were brought to nature preserves across Ukraine to reestablish the species. Some areas of Polissia are protected by the Emerald Network, an organization created to protect threatened habitats and species. By April 2021, breeding programs had increased the total Ukrainian population to approximately 350.[4]

**Ukraine is home to approximately 350 bird species, 100 mammal species, and 200 fish species.**[5]

## UKRAINE'S AQUATIC WILDLIFE

With numerous rivers and lakes and a border along the Black Sea, Ukraine has many aquatic plant and animal species. The Dnipro River is home to many different types of fish. Pike, perch, bream, catfish, and carp are just a few of the different families of fish that live in the Dnipro. Before reservoirs were built along the river, many river fish species lived in the Dnipro. Now many of those species have been replaced by lake species better suited to deeper, calmer water.

### THE CHERNOBYL EXCLUSION ZONE

In 1986, northern Ukraine was ground zero for one of the worst nuclear disasters in world history. A reactor at the Chernobyl nuclear plant exploded, releasing dangerous radiation into the environment. Since then, a 1,081-square-mile (2,800 sq km) area has been off-limits to humans. Now the Chernobyl Exclusion Zone is home to more than 60 rare species of mammals and birds, including wolves, lynx, bison, deer, bears, grouse, and wild boars.[7] Environmentalists consider it an accidental conservation success story.

Many other fish species can be found along Ukraine's coastline. With its low salt content and cold winters, the Black Sea is home to 150 native species, including cold-water fish such as herring, anchovies, and sprats.[6] The smallest Black Sea fish is the transparent goby, while the beluga sturgeon is the largest. Dolphins and porpoises also live in the Black Sea. Harbor porpoises migrate to the Sea of Azov in the spring.

Despite numerous rivers and miles of coastline, Ukraine's fish populations are in decline. Pollution from agricultural runoff and untreated sewage pollute Ukraine's rivers. The Pripet

**The Black Sea borders the southern parts of Ukraine, including the Crimean Peninsula. It is home to many different types of marine life, including dolphins and horse mackerel.**

Marshes in northern Ukraine and southern Belarus have been drained and transformed into agricultural land. This has altered the landscape and reduced habitat for the marshland's wildlife. Coastal water pollution has reduced seafood catches in the Black Sea and Sea of Azov too.

While pollution and other environmental concerns persist, Ukraine remains home to several important plant and animal habitats, from the Carpathian Mountains in the southwest to the Black Sea and Sea of Azov along the country's southern border. Conservation efforts have successfully preserved some of Ukraine's most important native species.

### CRIMEA'S THREATENED SPECIES

Several species native to the Crimean Peninsula are considered threatened. The Crimean rowan tree is native to just a few locations in the southern coast of the peninsula. An invasive wasp damages 99 percent of the tree's seeds before they can germinate into plants.[8] The Crimean stone grasshopper is an endangered insect that is native to Crimea and the surrounding area. It has lost its habitat to farming. An endangered hoverfly has also lost its habitat to development. The Crimea shemaya and Crimean Tatar goby are two endangered fish species native to the waters around the peninsula.

Catfish are common in Ukraine's many rivers, Including the Dnipro River.

CHAPTER **FOUR**

# HISTORY

Ukraine's wealth of natural resources has contributed to its long and often turbulent history. Its fertile steppe attracted early inhabitants as well as conflicts with outside powers that wanted to control Ukraine's natural bounty. Despite hundreds of years of outside pressure on their borders, the Ukrainian people persisted in their pursuit of an independent Ukraine.

Evidence of Ukraine's earliest inhabitants dates back about 150,000 years. Between 6000 and 2000 BCE, Neolithic Ukrainians progressed from hunter-gatherer communities to agricultural ones. The first agricultural settlements appeared northeast of the Carpathian Mountains along the Dnister River.

The National Museum of the Holodomor-Genocide in Kyiv seeks to educate people about the Holodomor genocide through its exhibits.

**Evidence of the Trypillians is shown through archeological objects such as decorated pottery and ceramic figurines.**

By 3500 BCE, communities had migrated east to settle along the Dnipro River in central Ukraine, where the fertile steppe made farming especially productive. Historians call these people the Trypillians. Between 3500 and 2700 BCE, communities of up to 700 Trypillians were common.[1] Trypillians were expert farmers. They invented a drill that bored holes in wood and stone and used wooden plows to cultivate their fields. Historians believe the Trypillians' success led to the civilization's decline and demise by 2000 BCE. Overcrowding may have pushed people to migrate north and east.

By 1500 BCE, horseback-riding nomads called the Cimmerians became the dominant inhabitants of Ukraine. The Cimmerians traded with metalworking people who lived in the Caucasus region southeast of modern-day Ukraine. This introduced iron to the people living on the Ukrainian steppe. Another civilization, called the Scythians, arrived from the east by 700 BCE. This nomadic civilization lived on the steppe north of the Black Sea. Like the Cimmerians, the Scythians were horseback-riding people. They created the first major organized civilization in Ukraine. Scythian elites forced other Scythians to pay them to prove their loyalty. Historians believe the Cimmerians and the Scythians competed and clashed with other groups for dominance on Ukraine's steppe.

Meanwhile, small colonies of Greek settlers had arrived along the Black Sea coast. Greek cities flourished along this coastline, including a cluster of cities on the Crimean Peninsula. After the transition to Roman rule in 63 BCE, the cities continued to exist for another 200 years, when they fell to military pressure from outside groups.

## KYIVAN RUS

As different groups competed for dominance on Ukraine's steppe and along its coast, smaller groups of people continued to live in the forested steppe of northern Ukraine. These farmers developed a culture and language of their own and are considered the first Slavs. Slavs today are the most numerous groups of people in Europe. They live in eastern and southeastern Europe, including Ukraine. The Slavs who live in Ukraine, Russia, and Belarus are East Slavs. In the 700s CE, East Slavs lived in the forests of northern and western Ukraine, spreading north and east from the Carpathian Mountains to the Pripet Marshes. Early East Slav communities were clusters of small villages with no central authority. However, by the late 700s CE, East Slav merchants consolidated their power in the town of Kyiv on the Dnipro River in what is now north-central Ukraine. As a river

**In his work, Sergey Vasilyevich Ivanov depicted the life of East Slavs. Ivanov was a Russian artist in the 1800s and was recognized for his historical paintings.**

city, Kyiv was the gateway between the Black Sea to the south and the Vikings to the north. The culture and political body that evolved from the trading city became known as Kyivan Rus.

By the late 900s CE, the Kyivan Rus state had expanded to include modern-day Lithuania, Latvia, and Estonia. Its southwestern border expanded to the Carpathian Mountains. Rather than having a central government, Kyivan Rus territory was governed by a number of small principalities. Over the next 300 years, various rulers from these principalities would dominate Kyivan Rus culture and trade.

The first and most prominent was Volodymyr the Great, who ruled between 980 and 1015 CE. During his reign, Volodymyr introduced the Kyivan Rus population to Christianity. He converted to Christianity to help establish stronger ties with the Christian Byzantine Empire. He had many residents of Kyiv baptized together in the Dnipro River in 988. At the same time, he destroyed sacred sites and idols from the pagan religions the Kyivan Rus people observed. He also sent 10 percent of the state's revenue to the Christian church in Constantinople.[2] These actions brought early Christianity to Kyivan Rus and paved the way for Ukrainians to become primarily Eastern Orthodox.

Volodymyr's son Yaroslav succeeded him in 1019. After Yaroslav's rule came to an end with his death in 1054, Kyivan Rus entered a long period of decline. This was due to a shift in trade routes from the Near East to Europe, conflicts between

**A bronze statue of Volodymyr the Great was erected in Kyiv in 1853.**

principalities, and war with other cultures on the Ukrainian steppe. In 1240, Kyiv was destroyed by Mongols after 20 years of persistent invasion. This marked the end of the Kyivan Rus. Ukraine was divided between three powers: the Mongols to the southeast, the grand duchy of Lithuania to the north, and the kingdom of Poland to the northwest.

## THREE POWERS

The Golden Horde was the western extension of Genghis Khan's empire. Genghis Khan was the ruler of Mongolia in Central Asia. He led troops west in search of more lands to conquer. In the mid-1300s, the southeast part of the Ukrainian steppe and the Crimean Peninsula were invaded and absorbed into Golden Horde territory. One hundred years later, the Golden Horde disintegrated. Its Ukrainian territory became part of the Crimean khanate. This state was under the influence of the Ottoman Empire, which included territory in North Africa and around the Black Sea and Red Sea. The Crimean khanate controlled southeast Ukraine until the Russian empire annexed the territory in 1783.

### GALICIA-VOLHYNIA

For a century after the fall of Kyivan Rus, the united principalities, Galicia and Volhynia, remained independent of Mongol, Lithuanian, or Polish rule. At the height of the two principalities' power in the 1200s, Galicia-Volhynia was home to about 90 percent of people who lived within Ukraine's modern borders.[3] Their leaders were wealthy and maintained strong militaries that fought off invasions from Poland and Hungary. Together, Galicia and Volhynia preserved elements of the culture and identity of Kyivan Rus, which would become an important part of Ukrainian national identity in the future.

**The Bakhchysaray Palace in Crimea was home to Crimean khans during the 1500s.**

Northwestern and central Ukraine faced another encroaching power: the grand duchy of Lithuania. Between the 1350s and 1360s, the duchy invaded and took over north-central Ukraine. This included Kyiv and other cities to the south. Eventually, Lithuania would claim most of Ukraine, the exception being the steppe in the southeast, the Crimean Peninsula, and the principality of Galicia.

Galicia became part of the kingdom of Poland in 1340. However, just 45 years later, Lithuania and Poland created an alliance through the Treaty of Krewo. This eventually formed the Polish-Lithuanian Commonwealth in 1569. During this time, Polish and Lithuanian culture influenced Ukraine. This included the introduction of Roman Catholicism. However, Ukrainians remained largely Eastern Orthodox despite pressure to convert. Around the same time, the Orthodox free peasants who farmed Ukrainian lands were being pressed into serfdom. This meant that the peasants' lands were given to wealthy Polish Roman Catholic landowners, and the peasants were required to work the land as a way of paying rent to their new landowners. For some peasants who lived along the southern border with the Crimean khanate, the injustice was too much to bear.

## RISE OF THE COSSACKS

By the 1400s, unhappy peasants and other people who opposed Polish-Lithuanian rule banded together in the southern frontier of the Polish-Lithuanian domain. They formed their own free society. Known as the Cossacks, from the Turkic *kazak*, or "free man," this group of people formed their own military and legislature. The Cossacks elected their military and political leaders. Over time, the Cossacks asserted their right to exist as their own state, rebelling against Polish rule. In 1620, they supported a new Orthodox hierarchy in Kyiv. With Cossack support, the Orthodox church ignited a cultural revival in Kyiv and influenced the founding of the first university in Ukraine, Kyivan Mohyla Academy.

**The Cossacks were known for their independent identity and military prowess. At times, the Russian Empire even used the Cossacks to defend its territory.**

In 1648, Cossack leader Bohdan Khmelnytsky led an uprising that quickly evolved into a popular rebellion of the peasants against the Polish state. Khmelnytsky marched to Kyiv in January 1649, declaring Ukraine an independent Cossack state. After years of warfare interrupted by shaky treaties with Poland, the conflict ended in 1658 with the Treaty of Hadyach. The treaty's terms established Rus as a self-governing duchy with the Cossack leader at its head. Rus would become an equal member of the Polish-Lithuanian Commonwealth.

Instead of bringing stability, however, the treaty kicked off years of competition between Cossack leaders. The treaty's terms were never implemented. Instead, a divide grew between the wealthy Cossack leaders and average Cossack soldiers and the peasantry. Ukraine under Cossack rule fell apart. In 1667, Ukraine was divided in half along the Dnipro River. The west side, called the Right Bank, went back to Polish rule. Kyiv and the east side, called the Left Bank, became part of Russia.

## UNDER IMPERIAL RULE

Between 1667 and 1795, the Polish-Lithuanian Commonwealth ruled the Right Bank of Ukraine. The Cossacks no longer influenced Ukrainian politics and culture. Instead, Polish elites took power. Ukrainian peasant farmers were pressed into serfdom under several powerful Polish landowners. Though several uprisings occurred over the decades of Polish rule, none succeeded in gaining independence for Ukrainians. In 1772, the Austro-Hungarian Empire annexed the province of Galicia. However, the region remained largely Ukrainian and Polish, and the Austro-Hungarian Empire left Polish elites in charge of Galicia. By 1914, Ukrainians in Galicia had made a few gains in education and culture, though they remained left out of political power.

In 1793 and 1795, the Russian Empire annexed the Right Bank and Volhynia province from the Polish-Lithuanian Commonwealth. This ended Polish control in Ukraine while expanding Russian control. After annexing the Crimean khanate territories in 1783, Russia embarked on the Russification of Ukraine. The Cossack nobility were given equal standing to the Russian nobility.

Meanwhile, peasant farmers once again were forced into serfdom, a condition that ended in 1861. Russia banned books in the Ukrainian language and forbade the language from being taught in schools. Despite this, a culture that valued education, literature, and the arts developed in Ukraine.

In 1917, three years after the start of World War I (1914–1918), peasants, workers, and soldiers revolted against the Russian Empire. The Russian Revolution of 1917 ended the empire. A group of socialist revolutionaries called the Bolsheviks took power. The Bolsheviks lifted the ban on the Ukrainian language and other restrictions on Ukrainians.

## UKRAINIAN REVOLUTION

Ukrainians took this opportunity to seek independence. Ukrainian political and

**The Russian Revolution was led by Vladimir Lenin, who became the head of the Soviet Union in 1917.**

professional groups formed the Central Rada, or Council, to represent their people. On November 7, 1917, the Central Rada declared it had authority over the new Ukrainian National Republic. This declaration put Ukraine in conflict with Bolshevik leaders, who declared Ukraine a Soviet republic under their new regime, the Union of Soviet Socialist Republics (USSR). The Central Rada pushed back a Bolshevik invasion of Kyiv with the help of German and Austrian forces. On January 22, 1918, it declared total independence for Ukraine.

However, just four months after its declaration of independence, the Central Rada was overthrown by General Pavlo Skoropadsky, a former Cossack supported by Germany. By October 1918, World War I was in its final weeks and Europe was in chaos. The breakdown of authority increased incidents of violence, especially against Ukraine's Jewish population. Between December 1918 and March 1921, Poland and the Soviets fought for control of Ukraine. In the aftermath of this conflict and the end of World War I, Ukraine was divided between four different states. The province of Bukovyna was annexed to Romania, and Transcarpathia was incorporated into the new country

### POGROMS IN UKRAINE

In the absence of a stable government after World War I, Ukraine experienced a rapid increase in violence. Much of this violence was directed at Ukraine's Jewish population. Jewish people had lived in Ukraine since the 1200s. Because they were perceived as part of the Polish ruling class, resentment against them sometimes erupted into violence. In 1918 and 1919, fighting forces in Ukraine organized pogroms, which were massacres of Jewish people. Tens of thousands of Jewish people were murdered by Ukrainian and Soviet soldiers as well as Ukrainian citizens.

of Czechoslovakia. Poland remained in control of Galicia and the western part of Volhynia. The rest of Ukraine formally became part of the USSR on December 30, 1922.

## SOVIET UKRAINE

Between 1921 and 1922, Soviet leaders struggled to get the USSR's economy off the ground. During the war, all industry had been brought under state management. Food was taken from some regions in the USSR, including Ukraine, to feed soldiers. On top of this, Ukraine experienced a drought. These factors led to a famine that killed more than three million Ukrainians.[4] By 1927, the USSR allowed private business and no longer forcibly took food from farmers. Ukraine's economy reached prewar levels. Between 1921 and 1928, the USSR adopted policies meant to appease its non-Russian citizens.

**Posters and other forms of propaganda distracted many people within the USSR from Joseph Stalin's acts of destruction.**

In Ukraine and other parts of the USSR, native languages were taught in schools and used in printed materials. In Ukraine, Ukrainian literature flourished.

However, life in Ukraine changed dramatically in 1928. That year, Soviet leader Joseph Stalin declared that peasants wealthy enough to own their own farms were enemies of the state. The Soviet government seized these peasants' property and deported them to Siberia or Kazakhstan. The Soviets created large, state-owned farms out of the seized property in a process called collectivization. Ninety percent of Ukraine's farmland was owned by the state by 1935.[5]

As part of collectivization, the Soviet government forcefully seized Ukraine's crops to feed people elsewhere in the USSR. They made it illegal for Ukraine's peasants to store food for themselves. Farmers could be shot for taking food to feed their families. As a result, Ukraine experienced a severe famine called the Holodomor between 1932 and 1933. Nearly four million Ukrainians died of preventable starvation. Meanwhile, the USSR exported more than one million short tons (907,185 metric tons) of grain to Europe.[6] It denied that any famine had occurred, banning any photographers or journalists from entering Ukraine during that time. This denial continued until the 1980s. This event was recognized as a genocide by Raphael Lemkin, a scholar who coined the term at a UN convention. Sixteen other countries, including the United States, recognize the human-caused Holodomor famine as an act of genocide.

Stalin also reversed the cultural freedom Ukraine and other Soviet states enjoyed in the 1920s. Soviet officials arrested church leaders and destroyed church property. They also arrested, deported, or killed Ukraine's writers, artists, and intellectual leaders. Historians estimate that by

Ukrainians remember the Holodomor genocide by lighting candles on the fourth Saturday of November.

the end of the 1930s, 80 percent of Ukraine's cultural leaders had been killed or repressed by the Soviet government.[7]

On September 1, 1939, Nazi Germany invaded Poland, starting World War II (1939–1945). The USSR took advantage of the invasion to incorporate western Ukraine into its territory. This region of Ukraine had been a part of Poland. Two years later, on June 22, 1941, German chancellor Adolf Hitler suddenly invaded the Soviet Union through Ukraine. By November, Ukraine was under Nazi control. At first, Ukrainians saw the Germans as liberators. But soon, the reality of the situation became clear. The Nazis took over the Ukrainian government and swiftly started a genocide against Ukraine's Jewish population. Approximately 1.5 million Ukrainian Jewish people were murdered by the Nazis between 1941 and 1944.[8]

**Ukraine spent about 70 years under Soviet rule.**

After a failed siege of the Soviet city of Stalingrad in 1943, the German army was forced to retreat west through Ukraine. By October 1944, the Soviet army had retaken possession of Ukraine, and Germany surrendered in May 1945. Between five and seven million Ukrainians had lost their lives in the war. More than ten million people were left homeless due to destruction in Ukraine's cities, towns, and villages.[9]

Despite these losses, the USSR put a new economic plan in place. The plan poured money into rebuilding Ukraine's heavy industries rather than its agricultural sector. This caused another famine between 1946 and 1947 that killed many Ukrainians. By 1950, Ukraine's economy was back to prewar levels.

After Stalin's death in 1953, the Soviet government reversed his policies of starvation, deportation, and execution. But his successors continued his policy of Russification between the 1950s and 1970s. The Ukrainian language was banned in schools and in print. In the 1970s and 1980s, Ukraine's economy faltered, as did many Soviet economies across the USSR. Then, in April 1986, one of the worst nuclear accidents in world history occurred in northern Ukraine. A reactor at the Chernobyl nuclear power plant experienced several explosions and fires. Because of radiation's lasting effects on health and the environment, the true impact of the accident may never be known.

The Chernobyl accident and subsequent Soviet mismanagement of the disaster renewed

**The Chernobyl disaster in 1986 is one of the worst nuclear accidents in history. An entire town had to be evacuated, and much of the area is still irradiated.**

# LEONID KRAVCHUK

Leonid Kravchuk served as Ukraine's first president between 1991 and 1994. In the 1980s, Kravchuk was the leader of Soviet Ukraine's propaganda and ideology departments. In this role, he controlled what information Ukrainians received and how it was distributed. These leadership roles catapulted him to head of the Ukrainian Supreme Soviet in 1990. As head of the Ukrainian Supreme Soviet, he was the leader of Soviet Ukraine.

Between 1990 and 1991, Kravchuk witnessed the USSR's central government weaken and the Ukrainian independence movement gain steam. He threw his support behind the independence movement and renounced his Communist Party membership. He became Ukraine's first democratically elected president in December 1991. Kravchuk passed away on May 10, 2022.

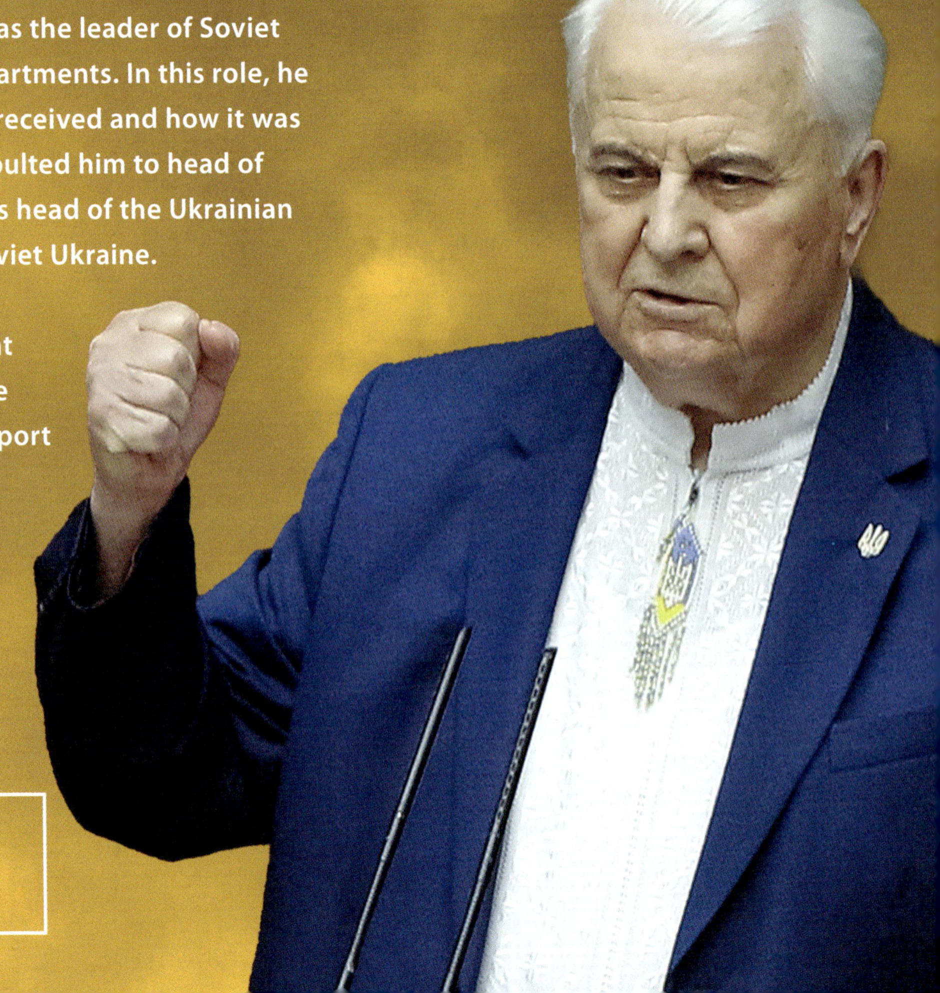

**Leonid Kravchuk was one of the three men who signed the declaration abolishing the Soviet Union in 1991.**

Ukrainian discontent with the Soviet government. Over the next few years, these sentiments grew into a call for Ukrainian independence.

## UKRAINIAN INDEPENDENCE

By 1991, the USSR was in decline. Many of the Soviet republics under its control moved to establish their independence. On December 1, 1991, Ukrainians went to the polls to decide whether to leave the Soviet Union. Ninety percent of voters supported independence.[10] Politician Leonid Kravchuk was elected president of newly independent Ukraine. The USSR itself dissolved on December 31, 1991. The former Soviet republics, including Russia, became independent.

In the first few years of independence, Kravchuk helped establish an independent military and government in Ukraine. The country adopted a pro-Western foreign policy that signaled Ukraine wanted to establish itself as a democracy and build economic ties with Europe. Bans on Ukraine's writers and intellectuals were lifted, as were restrictions on practicing religion.

### UKRAINIAN PRIDE

Ukraine achieved its independence in 1991. However, Ukrainians have been proud of their country long before then. In the 1800s, many Ukrainians wanted the right to rule themselves. They argued they had a unique language that was different from Russian or Polish. Since then, Ukrainians have fought for their right to exist as a nation. More recently, modern Ukrainians have embraced national pride. Many want Ukraine to be a strong, independent state where people want to live and work.

**While in office, Viktor Yanukovych, *right*, maintained close political connections with Russia's Vladimir Putin.**

Despite these efforts, Ukraine's economy grappled to find stability. Independence disrupted trade with Russia, which struggled to accept Ukraine's independence. The countries clashed over control of the Black Sea and the Crimean Peninsula. Russia raised prices on the energy it sold to Ukraine. Corruption within the Ukrainian government put more pressure on the economy. Over time, these factors boiled over into political upheaval.

The fight over corruption in Ukraine between pro-reform candidates and politicians who benefited from the corruption erupted in 2004. Prime Minister Viktor Yanukovych ran for president against opposition leader Viktor Yushchenko. Yanukovych was endorsed by the corrupt president, Leonid Kuchma, and received support from Russian president Vladimir Putin. During the presidential campaign, Yushchenko was poisoned in a supposed assassination attempt, leaving his face disfigured. Yushchenko and Yanukovych won equal amounts of the vote on October 31. A month later, a runoff election declared Yanukovych the winner.

Yushchenko's supporters claimed the runoff election was fraudulent and took to the streets in protest. They wore orange, which was Yushchenko's campaign color, and they protested for two weeks. The movement became known as the Orange Revolution. On December 3, 2004, Ukraine's Supreme Court ruled the election results were invalid. This triggered a second runoff election, which Yushchenko won on December 26.

Five years later, the 2010 presidential election turned the tables in Yanukovych's favor. He overwhelmingly won the election against incumbent Yushchenko. Yanukovych pursued friendlier relations with Russia, expanding an energy deal and dropping the former government's goal of joining the North Atlantic Treaty Organization (NATO).

In November 2013, under pressure from Russia, Yanukovych halted Ukraine's effort to build closer ties with the European Union. The move prompted massive protests in Kyiv. Despite police violently breaking up crowds, the protests continued into December. In January, the protests evolved into riots, with demonstrators and police clashing violently. Yanukovych passed a series of laws restricting the right to protest, which backfired, as hundreds of thousands of people responded in protest in the streets of Kyiv. In February, the military forcibly took back the city's center. Dozens of people were killed, and hundreds were injured.

On February 21, Yanukovych and opposition leaders reached an agreement. Ukraine's legislature officially pardoned protesters, fired Yanukovych's internal affairs minister, and voted to

In 2014, many Ukrainians took to the streets of Kyiv to protest against Vladimir Putin's move to invade the Crimean Peninsula.

impeach Yanukovych. Yanukovych fled to Russia shortly before the vote. Oleksandr Turchynov was appointed interim president until an early presidential election in May 2014.

## NEW CHALLENGES TO INDEPENDENT UKRAINE

Russia took advantage of the chaos of the Maidan protest movement and political upheaval. In February and March 2014, Russian soldiers entered the Crimean Peninsula and surrounded its airports. These soldiers did not wear Russian military uniforms, but military intelligence proved that the troops were Russian and directed by Putin. Gunmen occupied the Crimean government building and raised the Russian flag. On March 16, Crimean voters chose to leave Ukraine and become a part of Russia. Analysis of the vote revealed irregularities with the process, including soldiers patrolling polling stations. Western leaders condemned Russia's invasion and the illegitimate vote. Russia's occupation of Crimea continued through at least 2022, though its claim to the peninsula is rejected by most of the world.

By the presidential election of 2019, Ukrainians had grown tired of the conflict with Russia in the southeast, a struggling economy, and government corruption. In March 2019, Ukrainians overwhelmingly elected Volodymyr Zelenskyy as their next president. Zelenskyy was new to politics and had been a television star. His political party was named after his popular sitcom *Servant of the People*. In the show, Zelenskyy played a teacher who suddenly becomes president. Zelenskyy promised to curb corruption and pursue a peace deal with Russia. He could not have anticipated that three years later, he would face Ukraine's greatest threat yet. In February 2022, Russia launched a large-scale invasion of Ukraine from the north, east, and south.

CHAPTER **FIVE**

# PEOPLE AND CULTURE

Despite centuries of occupation, a distinctly Ukrainian culture has persisted. This has been especially true in the decades after the fall of the USSR. Since then, Ukrainians have worked hard to build a national identity that unites the estimated 43.5 million people who call Ukraine home.[1]

Since independence in 1991, Ukraine has experienced an overall decline in population. The number of Ukrainians being born couldn't keep up with the number of people dying or migrating from the country. Millions of Ukrainians live and work outside Ukraine in Russia or nations in the European Union.

Kalush Orchestra represented Ukraine in the 2022 Eurovision Song Contest. After their win, the group sold its first-place trophy in an auction to raise money for Ukraine war aid.

Russia's invasion of Ukraine in 2022 also contributed to the declining population, as millions of refugees fled to neighboring countries.

More than 77 percent of Ukrainians identify as ethnically Ukrainian. Approximately 17 percent identify as Russian. Together, these two ethnicities make up about 95 percent of the Ukrainian population. Other ethnic groups living in Ukraine include Crimean Tatars, Bulgarians, Hungarians, Romanians, Polish people, and Jewish people. Each of these groups represents less than 1 percent of Ukraine's total population.[2]

**By July 4, 2022, more than 12 million Ukrainians had fled the country since Russia began its invasion in February 2022.[4]**

Ukraine's national language is Ukrainian, which is part of the Slavic language family. Ukrainian is written in the Cyrillic alphabet, a writing system developed in the 800s to 900s CE. Russian, Serbian, and more than 50 other languages also use the Cyrillic alphabet. Most Ukrainians speak Ukrainian as their primary language. However, nearly 30 percent of Ukrainians speak Russian as their primary language.[3]

A small minority of Ukrainians speak Crimean Tatar, Moldovan, Romanian, or another language as their primary tongue. During Russification, the Ukrainian language was banned in schools and other public places. Today, all schools teach in Ukrainian, and many Russian speakers are learning the language as a way to express their Ukrainian identity.

## URBAN AND RURAL, RICH AND POOR

Nearly 70 percent of Ukrainians live in an urban center.[5] Kyiv in north-central Ukraine has the largest population of any city in the nation. Approximately three million people live in Kyiv. Kharkiv is a city in northeast Ukraine, on the country's border with Russia. It is home to more than 1.4 million people.[6] These cities are highly industrialized. They attract workers seeking employment and a higher standard of living. Other large cities include Odesa, a coastal city on the Black Sea, and Dnipro, a city along the Dnipro River in southeast Ukraine.

While most Ukrainians live in cities, others live in Ukraine's rural communities. More than half of Ukraine's rural population live in villages of 1,000 to 5,000 residents.[7] Most rural Ukrainians are employed in the agricultural industry as farmers or other workers.

In addition to the difference between Ukraine's urban and rural populations, there is a large divide between its richest and poorest residents. Oligarchs are very rich business owners who have political power. Many became much wealthier after Ukraine became independent in 1991. Oligarchs control

### THE HUTSULS

The Hutsuls are a group of highlanders who live in the Carpathian Mountains. They were first identified as a separate ethnic group in the 1700s. The Hutsuls speak their own dialect of the Ukrainian language. They are known for their wooden churches and colorful traditional clothing. Hutsul handicrafts include ceramics, embroidered clothing and pillows, rugs, and decorated leather.

airlines, banks, media companies, and entire industries. They have their own television stations and political parties. They live lavish lifestyles and own properties abroad. Many pay corrupt judges and legislators to use their political power to make the oligarchs richer. When President Zelenskyy took office in 2019, he promised to reduce the power and number of oligarchs in Ukraine. He created a list of 13 oligarchs whose business empires he wished to dismantle. However, he made little progress in this task before Ukraine was invaded by Russia in February 2022.

While a few extremely rich businesspeople control much of Ukraine's media and industry, most Ukrainians are in the working class. In 2018, highly skilled workers in Ukraine made an average of $214 a month. Low-skilled workers in Ukraine made an average of $137 a month.[8] Many middle-class Ukrainians work multiple jobs, and it is common for Ukrainians living outside cities to grow their own food.

## UKRAINIAN WOMEN

Attitudes toward women in Ukraine remain tied to traditional gender roles and norms. The majority of both men and women support traditional roles for women, such as being caregivers, nurses, and teachers. However, women are less likely than men to accept stereotypes about women, such as women's emotions affecting their ability to make good decisions. Many Ukrainian women face discrimination in the workforce. Age, family situation, and appearance persist as factors in securing a well-paying job. On average, Ukrainian women earn 26 percent less money than men in the same role do.[9]

After Russia's invasion in 2022, many Ukrainian women stayed to help refugees by supplying food to those remaining in the country.

However, many women are working to move Ukraine's views on women forward. In 2008, economist Anna Hutsol founded the FEMEN movement. This group of radical feminists protests governments that oppress women and fights to end sex trafficking. The FEMEN movement also seeks to separate religion from government to protect the reproductive rights of women. In 2022, the Russian invasion of Ukraine brought a new change to traditional gender roles. While millions of women and children fled the fighting, many women stayed to fight. In March 2022, approximately 30,000 women had enlisted in the Ukrainian army.[10] Thousands of other women stayed to support the troops by supplying food, medical supplies, and camouflage.

## PRACTICING RELIGION IN UKRAINE

Despite a decades-long Soviet ban on the Ukrainian Catholic and Orthodox Churches in the 1900s, Ukraine's long-observed religious traditions survived. In 2022, about two-thirds of all Ukrainians identified as Orthodox. Another 10 percent identified as Ukrainian Greek Catholic, and small minorities practiced Protestantism, Judaism, or Islam.[11]

Eastern Orthodoxy is the dominant religion in Ukraine. The Orthodox Catholic Church is a type of Christianity popular in Eastern Europe and the Middle East. Followers of the Ukrainian Orthodox Church choose to follow one of two different patriarchates. A patriarchate is the office of the top leader of the church. For 300 years, the Ukrainian Orthodox Church had just one patriarchate, which was based in Moscow, Russia. In 2019, the Kyiv Patriarchate became independent from the Moscow Patriarchate. This new organization is based in Kyiv, Ukraine. Most followers of the

**Saint Andrew's Church is an Orthodox church in Kyiv, notable for its Baroque-style architecture and elegance.**

Moscow Patriarchate live in southern and eastern Ukraine, where Russian influence is strong. Most followers of the Kyiv Patriarchate live in central and western Ukraine.

Other Ukrainians are members of the Ukrainian Greek Catholic Church. This is the largest branch of the Eastern Catholic Church, a part of the Roman Catholic Church. Many followers of this religion live in western Ukraine. Although Muslims make up a small population of Ukraine, Islam has history that stems back to the 1300s when the religion was introduced by Mongol rulers. Today, Islam is commonly practiced by Crimean Tatars on the Crimean Peninsula in southern Ukraine. Before World War II, Ukraine was home to the Soviet Union's largest Jewish community. But between June 1941 and May 1945, an estimated 1.5 million Jewish people were murdered by German soldiers, approximately 60 percent of Ukraine's Jewish population before the war.[12] Today, less than 1 percent of Ukrainians practice Judaism.[13]

## VISUAL ARTS AND LITERATURE

Christianity has influenced traditional Ukrainian visual art since the 900s CE. Pieces of religious artwork, including mosaics and sacred images called icons, adorn many cathedrals and churches. The Cathedral of Saint Sophia in Kyiv contains mosaics and frescoes from the 1000s and 1100s. Other churches containing religious artwork were destroyed by Soviet authorities in the 1930s.

Ukrainians are also known for their folk art. Wood carvings, embroidery, ceramics, and weavings are highly ornamental and vary in style by region. A popular example is *pysanky*, Easter eggs designed with bright colors and intricate patterns.

Despite efforts to silence the Ukrainian language, the country has a rich literary heritage. In the 1700s and 1800s, writers contributed to the Ukrainian national identity. Ivan Kotlyarevsky was a poet and playwright in the late 1700s. In the play *Eneyida*, he reimagined Virgil's *Aeneid*, an ancient Roman epic poem. Kotlyarevsky featured the Ukrainian Cossacks instead of Virgil's Greek heroes. In the mid-1800s, Taras Hryhorovych Shevchenko started writing poems about Ukraine's history, including its oppression by Russia. While writers struggled to create works under Soviet rule due to strict rules on the type of writing permitted, freedom of expression blossomed after independence in 1991. Today, Ukrainians create and read newspapers, literary journals, novels, and nonfiction books.

### TARAS SHEVCHENKO, NATIONAL POET

Taras Hryhorovych Shevchenko was born on March 9, 1814, in a small village in central Ukraine. At the time, Ukraine was part of the Russian Empire. Born a serf, Shevchenko was freed from serfdom while he was a student at the Saint Petersburg Academy of Art. His poems, including the long poem *Haidamaky*, focused on Ukrainian history and national identity. In 1847, Shevchenko was punished for writing a series of poems that criticized Russia's oppression of Ukraine. He was exiled and forced into military service. Shevchenko died in Saint Petersburg, Russia, on March 10, 1861, a day after his 47th birthday.

## RICH MUSICAL HERITAGE

Like folk art, folk music is a popular pastime in Ukraine. Singers may perform historical songs, or *dumy*, without instrumental accompaniment

**Hopak is Ukraine's national dance. The dance incorporates a lot of high jumps, squats, kicks, and leaps.**

or while strumming a lute-like instrument called a bandura. Folk dancers in the countryside may perform a hopak, an energetic dance. In the early 2000s, these moves became incorporated into a Ukrainian martial arts technique called combat hopak.

Ukraine also has a rich classical and pop music tradition. Opera was a popular musical form during the 1800s, and vocal works became common in the early 1900s. Mykola Lysenko was a well-known composer in the early 1900s. He wrote operas, choral works, and piano pieces. In the late 1900s, many Ukrainians started to enjoy listening to pop music. In the 1990s, rock, ska, and punk artists topped the charts. In 2004, Ukrainian singer Ruslana Lyzhychko won the Eurovision Song Contest. Ukraine also won Eurovision in 2022 with Kalush Orchestra, a group that blended Ukraine's traditional music and art with hip-hop sounds. Rapper Alyona Alyona's debut album *Ribki* became a big hit in Ukraine and across Europe in 2018. Since then, she has won three international awards for her music.

## UKRAINIAN CUISINE

While international options such as pizza and Greek and Chinese food are increasingly common in Ukraine, many continue to enjoy the country's traditional cuisine. These foods include golubtsi, or stuffed cabbage rolls, a popular family dish. *Borshch* is a traditional dish enjoyed by many families too. It is a thick stew made of beetroot, cabbage, potatoes, onions, carrots, and a protein such as pork, veal, or chicken. Ukrainians add a dollop of sour cream to their borshch and serve it with garlic rolls called *pampushky*.

**Beet is the main ingredient in borshch. This vegetable gives the soup its flavor and bright red color.**

Boiled dumplings called *varenyky* have been popular in Ukraine for centuries. They are mentioned in Ukrainian literature and folk songs and included in many families' Christmas celebrations. Varenyky are typically stuffed with potatoes, mushrooms, cabbage, or meat, though sweet versions are also becoming common. Raw pig fat, or *salo*, is another traditional Ukrainian food. Ukrainian restaurants may offer salo smoked, flavored with garlic and salt, or dipped in chocolate.

## SOCCER AND OTHER NATIONAL PASTIMES

Sports are an important pastime for many Ukrainians. Soccer is the country's national sport. Many Ukrainians are fans of one of the 12 teams that play in the Ukrainian Premier League, as well as the national team. Boxing, tennis, and ice hockey are also popular sports that many people follow and enjoy participating in. The Klitschko brothers are two successful boxers from Ukraine who have competed internationally. Men and women play tennis recreationally and at a professional level. Ice hockey is a beloved pastime in the colder months. Chess is popular in Ukraine and is considered a sport in the country. Many Ukrainians also enjoy spending time hiking, cycling, swimming, and skiing in nature reserves and parks.

### VITALI AND WLADIMIR KLITSCHKO, BOXING BROTHERS

Vitali and Wladimir Klitschko are brothers who have overcome challenges throughout their lives. They grew up just 60 miles (97 km) from the Chernobyl nuclear plant.[14] When they were young, their father was called to respond to the disaster. Both brothers earned multiple boxing heavyweight world champion titles during their boxing careers. After retiring at age 41, Vitali was elected mayor of Kyiv. In February 2022, both brothers enlisted in the Ukrainian army to defend the country against Russian invasion.

Centuries of foreign occupation and oppression did not prevent Ukrainians from developing and celebrating a distinct national identity and culture. Since gaining its independence in 1991, Ukraine has attempted to bridge the divide between super-rich and average Ukrainians and improve the treatment of women. While doing so, Ukrainians have maintained the art, food, and cultural traditions that make Ukraine a distinct and unique nation.

CHAPTER **SIX**

# POLITICS

When Ukrainians voted to become an independent nation in 1991, it set in motion the creation of a constitution that would guide the formation of an independent government. The constitution went into effect in 1996. It replaced the Soviet constitution that had been in place while Ukraine was part of the USSR.

The new constitution created the structure for Ukraine's legislative, executive, and judicial branches of government. The country has a unicameral legislature known as the Verkhovna Rada, or Supreme Council of Ukraine. Each legislator belongs to one of Ukraine's many political parties. Citizens 18 years or older can vote. During parliamentary elections, citizens can vote for a political party and an individual candidate to

The Verkhovna Rada building in Kyiv is where Ukraine's parliament meets for its sessions.

Denys Shmyhal began serving as Ukraine's prime minister on March 4, 2020.

represent their district. This system, called proportional representation, ensures minority parties are represented in the legislature. Ukraine adopted this system in 2004.

The president is the head of state in Ukraine and serves a five-year term. A direct popular vote elects the president. The president oversees the executive branch of the government and has the power to veto legislation. He or she is the commander in chief of the armed forces and heads the National Security and Defense Council. The president appoints a prime minister, who is the head of the government. The prime minister is typically the leader of the majority party in the legislature. The legislature confirms the president's choice. Together, the president and prime minister appoint members of the cabinet. Cabinet members are in charge of daily government operations.

The Supreme Court of Ukraine is the highest court in the country. Its 48 judges supervise the activities of the lower courts. There is also the Constitutional Court of Ukraine that decides cases related to constitutional matters. Typically, 18 judges oversee cases related to the constitutionality of laws.

## HOW A PARLIAMENTARY SYSTEM WORKS

Ukraine's legislature operates on a parliamentary system. In this system, parties with the highest number of seats in the legislature are in charge of the government. Sometimes, parties must create partnerships, called coalitions, with other parties in order to govern. Minority parties often challenge the proposed laws and decisions of the ruling party or coalition. The ruling party leader becomes the prime minister. Prime ministers can be removed with a vote of no confidence. The ruling party or minority parties may call for a vote of no confidence to remove a prime minister.

Ukraine is a unitary republic that consists of 24 oblasts, or provinces. As a unitary republic, the national government creates, executes, and interprets the law for the entire country. Civil servants in the oblasts implement the national law. This is similar to how the government works at the state level in the United States, where states have legislatures, governors, and state courts that create, execute, and interpret state laws. US state civil servants at the county and local levels implement these laws.

## UKRAINE'S POLITICAL PARTIES

Ukraine's government is a multiparty system. This offers voters many options for representation. Some parties are conservative, while others are progressive or centrist in ideology. Some parties have formed around specific ideas, such as communism. Not all parties win enough votes to become the majority party in the Verkhovna Rada. It is common for minority parties to work together or merge to grow their power in the legislature.

### THE AUTONOMOUS REPUBLIC OF CRIMEA

The Crimean Peninsula is home to an ethnic minority group called the Crimean Tatars. Tatars are the Muslim descendants of the Golden Horde in the 1200s. As a region with a large minority population, Crimea was declared an autonomous republic under the Soviet Union. In 1944, Joseph Stalin forcibly deported the Crimean Tatars for allegedly cooperating with the Nazis. After Stalin's death and the fall of the Soviet Union, Crimea eventually became a part of independent Ukraine, and many Tatars returned to Crimea.

However, in 2014, Russia laid claim to Crimea and invaded the region, occupying it ever since.

# VOLODYMYR ZELENSKYY

Volodymyr Zelenskyy is an actor and comedian who was elected president of Ukraine in 2019. Born in 1978 in southern Ukraine, he studied law at Kyiv National Economic University. While there, he started acting in the theater department. In October 2015, Zelenskyy starred in the popular sitcom *Servant of the People*, which was about a teacher who goes viral for a passionate speech against corruption. Eventually, the teacher is elected president of Ukraine.

The success of the show led to the formation of the Servant of the People political party. Zelenskyy became the party's presidential candidate in 2018. During his time in office, Zelenskyy tried to reduce corruption in the Ukrainian government. He also led the country's response to the COVID-19 pandemic as well as Russia's invasion of Ukraine.

**During the war with Russia, President Zelenskyy wore simple green T-shirts to show solidarity with Ukraine's soldiers.**

Ukrainian service members march in a military parade on August 24, the Independence Day of Ukraine.

In 2022, the Servant of the People Party was the ruling party in the Verkhovna Rada. This was the party of President Volodymyr Zelenskyy. It was named after Zelenskyy's popular sitcom, *Servant of the People*, which satirized Ukraine's government. Other parties include the Rukh, or Popular Movement of Ukraine, the Social Democratic Party, and Svoboda Party. The Orange Revolution gave birth to several pro-Western parties, including Yushchenko's Our Ukraine—People's Self-Defense Bloc and Batkivshchyna. In March 2022, the Verkhovna Rada passed a law banning political parties that promote Russia, including the Opposition Platform—For Life party. This party is popular in eastern Ukraine, where support for Russia is high.

## UKRAINIAN MILITARY MIGHT

When Ukraine became independent in 1991, it inherited approximately 750,000 Soviet troops and 5,000 nuclear weapons.[1] It required the troops to swear an oath of loyalty to independent Ukraine. Those who refused were given funds to leave the country. Over the next few years, Ukraine reduced its standing military by several hundred thousand members. In the early 1990s, Soviet nuclear weapons that were left in Ukraine's territory were transferred to Russia. In exchange, the United

States, United Kingdom, and Russia agreed to guarantee Ukraine's security. In 1994, Ukraine signed the Treaty on the Non-Proliferation of Nuclear Weapons, an international agreement. That year, Ukraine also began a broader effort to significantly reduce its arsenal of weapons, ammunition, and other military assets.

**In February 2022, Ukraine's military included 145,000 army, 45,000 air force, and 11,000 navy personnel.[2]**

In September 2014, Ukraine signed an agreement with Lithuania and Poland that established a joint military brigade. The brigade is called the LITPOLUKRBRIG. The LITPOLUKRBRIG responds to crises and humanitarian situations in Lithuania, Poland, and Ukraine. Troops are stationed in their home countries and are on standby to be called to duty.

## IMPORTANT SYMBOLS

Ukraine has several national symbols that help unify the country under a shared identity and culture. The flag of Ukraine is two equal horizontal bars of blue and yellow. The blue appears above the yellow. The two colors have been associated with Ukraine for centuries. Modern interpretations of the flag claim the colors represent grain fields under the sky. Sometimes, Ukraine's coat of arms, the *tryzub*, is displayed with the flag. The tryzub is a gold trident often displayed on a blue background. It was the coat of arms of the Kyivan Rus.

The national anthem of Ukraine is "Shche ne vmerla Ukrainy," or "Ukraine Has Not Yet Perished." It was adopted by the Verkhovna Rada in 1992. However, the melody and lyrics of the national anthem were written in the 1860s and first recorded in the 1910s, when Ukraine was under Russian rule.

### THE TRYZUB

The Verkhovna Rada adopted the tryzub as the Small State Emblem of Ukraine in 1992. Four years later, its status as one of Ukraine's national symbols was added to the constitution. The tryzub was briefly used as independent Ukraine's coat of arms in 1918, before the country was folded into the USSR. Many theories try to explain the symbolism of the tryzub. Some people say it represents the Christian holy trinity. Others say it represents a bow and arrows, an anchor, or a candlestick.

Ukraine also has several important cultural symbols and objects. The sunflower is Ukraine's national flower, and its national fruit is the cherry. The common nightingale is the national animal, and the viburnum is the country's national tree. Ukraine's national dish is borshch. These symbols and objects help unite the country as a single nation.

CHAPTER **SEVEN**

# ECONOMICS

Since gaining independence from the Soviet Union in 1991, Ukraine has struggled to build a thriving economy. Corruption is a major reason Ukraine's economy lags behind other former Soviet and Soviet-influenced countries. According to Ukraine's National Reform Council, corruption costs the economy $37 billion every year.[1] The Ministry of Economic Development and Trade estimated that 31 percent of Ukraine's economy in 2020 was conducted outside tax and regulatory laws.[2]

Since 2014, the country has worked to reduce corruption in the government and its economy, including breaking up the monopolies Ukraine's oligarchs have on various industries. Starting in 2016, the country has required civil servants to report their

Ukraine is known as the "breadbasket of Europe," as the country is a major exporter of wheat, corn, and sunflower oil.

Vladimir Vernadsky founded the Ukrainian Academy of Sciences.

assets every year. This helps uncover imbalances between a civil servant's income and lifestyle, a sign of potential corruption. Reducing corruption in Ukraine would create more wealth for the country and its citizens as a whole.

## CURRENCY

**In 2017, Ukraine's national annual revenue was $29.82 billion.[4]**

Ukraine's official currency is the hryvnia. Its name comes from a decoration people wore on their necks during the Kyivan Rus times. After Ukraine gained its independence in 1991, it became important for the nation to create its own form of currency. In September 1996, the hryvnia was officially introduced to Ukrainians. On the same day, coins, called kopiyka, were also put into circulation.

The modern 1,000-hryven note is the most circulated denomination. Vladimir Vernadsky, a well-known philosopher and scientist, is featured on the front of this note. On the back of the 1,000-hryven note is the building of the National Academy of Sciences of Ukraine.

## AGRICULTURE IN CENTRAL AND WESTERN UKRAINE

While just 5.8 percent of its workforce is involved in agriculture, Ukraine is a major producer of various farm crops.[3] It outpaces most other European countries in its production of potatoes and grains, such as wheat, barley, corn, and oats. Additionally, Ukraine is one of the world's top producers of sugar beets and sunflower oil. Farmers on the Crimean Peninsula grow grapes for winemaking, while farmers in the foothills of the Carpathian Mountains grow lots of potatoes. The fertile steppe of central Ukraine is ideal for growing sunflowers, flax, hemp, poppy seeds, tomatoes, and peppers. Farmers across Ukraine also raise livestock, including cattle, hogs, sheep, goats, and poultry.

In addition to farming, forestry and fishing are important industries in the country. The forested steppe of northern and western Ukraine provides lumber and other wood products. The State Forest Resources Agency manages the country's forestry industry. Ukraine's rivers and southern coast support the country's fishing industry. The Black Sea and Sea of Azov provide seafood, while Ukraine's major rivers, such as the Dnipro and Dnister, provide freshwater fish. However, water pollution has caused a decline in the productivity of Ukraine's fishing industry.

## FEEDING THE WORLD

Ukraine's agricultural industry feeds the world. In 2021, it was the second-largest supplier of grains to Europe.[5] Countries including Egypt, Bangladesh, and Moldova get a majority of their grain from Ukraine. That same year, Ukraine was the world's largest exporter of sunflower oil.[6] China, India, the Netherlands, Spain, and Italy are top importers of Ukrainian sunflower oil. Russia's invasion in 2022 interrupted Ukraine's agricultural industry. Economists feared many people around the world would go hungry without food imports from Ukraine.

Kryvyy Rih is a major iron ore deposit in eastern Ukraine. It plays a significant role in the country's economy.

**In 2014, 67.8 percent of the Ukrainian workforce had service jobs, 26.5 percent had industrial jobs, and 5.8 percent had agricultural jobs.[7]**

## HEAVY INDUSTRY IN EASTERN UKRAINE

The steppe of eastern Ukraine is rich in minerals, making mining and related industries important economic drivers in the region. Southeastern Ukraine contains rich iron ore veins that supply the country's iron and steel industries. Its steel industry is one of the most productive in the world. Ukraine's iron and steel are turned into cast iron, rolled steel, and steel pipe in ironworks in the Donbas region in the east. These materials are turned into heavy equipment, such as turbines and generators, and modes of transportation, such as locomotives, freight cars, and ships. They are also used to manufacture military equipment, much of which is exported to Russia, China, and Pakistan.

Ukraine's eastern region also supplies much of the country's energy. Coal, natural gas, and petroleum are all mined or produced in central and eastern Ukraine. However, the country does not produce enough energy on its own to meet its needs. It imports oil and natural gas from Russia to make up the difference.

## UKRAINE'S SERVICE SECTOR

While agriculture and heavy industry are important to the economy, most Ukrainians work service jobs. These jobs are located in urban centers and in the countryside. Many Ukrainians work in

**Odesa's main railway station offers direct trains to Ukraine's major cities.**

the country's transportation and communications industries. Others work jobs related to tourism. The southern coast of Crimea is a popular vacation spot, as are the country's natural reserves in the Carpathian Mountains. Since 2011, Ukraine has allowed visitors to tour Pryp'yat, the site of the Chernobyl nuclear disaster in northern Ukraine.

### SOVIET ECONOMIC LEGACY

Ukraine's history as part of the USSR left many marks on its modern economy. Ukraine was a top-producing member of the Soviet Union, but much of the wealth it generated was invested elsewhere in the USSR. After independence, Ukraine had to manage the bankruptcy of Soviet-run industries. Private businesses bought entire industries, from grocery stores to steel mills. This created an oligarchy that controlled most of Ukraine's economy.

## TRANSPORTATION AND TELECOMMUNICATIONS INFRASTRUCTURE

Ukraine relies on highways, railways, and airports to move people and goods across its landscape. Major cities are connected by highways and railways. Ukraine's rail network is especially robust in its eastern region, where it supports Ukraine's heavy industry. Most major cities have airports with airlines that fly within Ukraine and around the world. Seaports support shipping along Ukraine's southern coast too.

Since 1991, Ukraine has worked to upgrade its Soviet-era telecommunications infrastructure. Obsolete telephone systems have been replaced with fiber-optic and satellite systems. A robust cellular network connects mobile devices across the country. Ukraine has also invested in its

### THE WORLD'S FIRST POSTAL CODE

Today, postal codes are common in the United States and across the world. But the postal code system was invented in Ukraine in the 1930s. Ukraine's first postal code assigned unique codes to towns, villages, and railway stations. The system was implemented in December 1932 in Kharkiv and quickly spread across Ukraine. Residents received postcards explaining the system and how to write mailing addresses with the codes. The system stopped abruptly in the summer of 1939, as rumors of war in Europe grew.

internet access, making Wi-Fi prevalent in cities and on public transportation.

Television is an important part of daily life and provides most Ukrainians with their news, though social media is an increasingly popular news source. Most of Ukraine's news outlets are owned by oligarchs, and many have obvious political leanings. An exception is the state-owned National Public Broadcasting Company of Ukraine. Though less popular, its coverage is more balanced than other news outlets.

Ukraine is rich in natural resources. These resources are the backbone of its economy, and service-related jobs are on the rise too. If anti-corruption efforts are successful, Ukraine may be able to improve its economy and the standard of living for everyday people.

CHAPTER **EIGHT**

# UKRAINE TODAY

Ukrainian daily life is as varied as anywhere else in the world. In Kyiv, most people live in apartment towers. Many apartment buildings date back to the Soviet era but have been remodeled and modernized. Though these apartments may be small, people in Kyiv often live with extended family members. Many families invest in a couple of modern conveniences, such as a large television or a new washing machine.

A typical day may start with a bowl of kasha, or buckwheat porridge. After that, people may stop by their local café for a latte on their walk to work or school. Walking is the preferred way to get around,

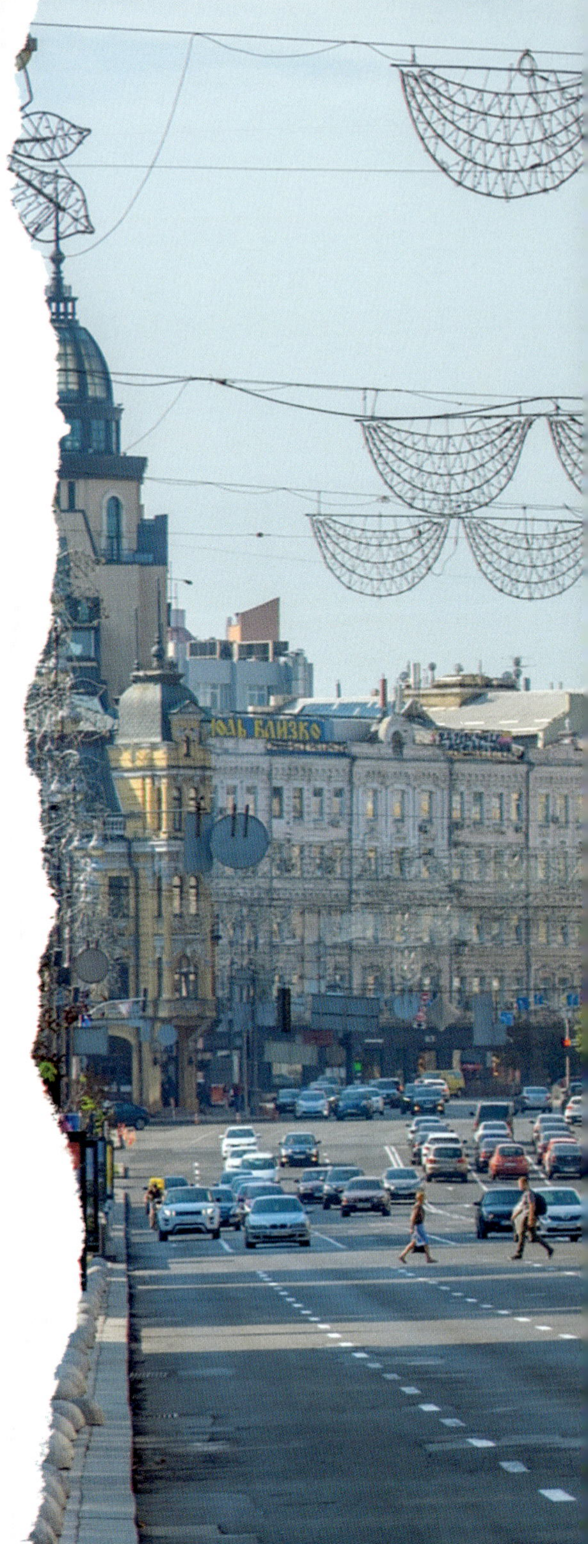

Khreshchatyk is Kyiv's main street. It includes many shopping areas, cafés, restaurants, and street vendors.

though Kyiv and other cities do offer buses, trolleys, trams, and subways. In Ukraine, students attend school for 12 years. They spend four years in elementary school, five years in middle school, and three years in secondary school. They may attend a public school or private or religious school. Since 1991, schools have incorporated Ukrainian literature and history into their curricula.

Once their 12 years of school are complete, students can decide to start work or continue their education at a university. Ukraine has a strong culture of higher education. Many of the institutions operating today were established in the 1800s. Most cities have at least one university, and public and private higher education are available across the country.

After school or work, students and their families have lots of options for recreation. Many cities have parks that Ukrainians enjoy walking through or picnicking in. Cafés, shops, and kiosks offer places to shop. A family might spend an evening at their city's opera house. Young people might visit their local dance club. Or they may watch the latest American blockbuster at the local movie theater. Most young Ukrainians are avid social media and

## UKRAINE'S RESPONSE TO COVID-19

In 2020, the COVID-19 pandemic caused major disruptions in Ukrainian daily life. The country went into lockdown, and non-essential businesses were forced to shut their doors. Fighting in the Donbas region had damaged the water supply infrastructure, making medical care and hygiene difficult. By the spring of 2022, five million Ukrainians had been infected with COVID-19, and more than 108,500 people had died of the disease. Approximately 35.7 percent of the population had been vaccinated.[1]

During their free time, families in Odesa might go to the National Academic Opera and Ballet Theater, the oldest opera house in Ukraine, to watch ballet or opera performances.

smartphone users. With Wi-Fi available most places, it is common to see teenage Ukrainians hanging out with their phones in hand.

**In 2022, 69.9 percent of Ukrainians lived in a city.[2]**

## WHISPERS OF WAR

Cellphones and social media helped keep Ukrainians of all ages informed in the run-up to the Russian invasion in February 2022. In October 2021, news outlets on television and social media

Before Vladimir Putin announced the invasion of Ukraine on February 24, he made an address to Russia, saying that he would decide to recognize the independence of Ukraine's rebel provinces.

started reporting that Russian troops were gathering along Ukraine's northeastern border. Though troubling, Russian aggression was nothing new to Ukrainians. Since Russia's occupation of the Crimean Peninsula in 2014, pro-Russian separatists in the Donbas region of southeast Ukraine had attacked Ukrainian cities in an effort to gain control of the region. The Ukrainian government and Western nations accused Russia of directly supporting the separatists.

By February 2022, Russia had gathered approximately 190,000 troops along the border with Ukraine.[3] Russian warships conducted exercises in the Black Sea. Western leaders warned President Zelenskyy that an invasion appeared to be looming. Russian president Vladimir Putin denied these claims, saying the troops and warships were involved in scheduled exercises and nothing more. However, it soon became clear that Putin had lied about his intentions.

## FEBRUARY 24, 2022

On February 21, 2022, Putin made a formal announcement recognizing the independence of the Donbas oblasts of Donetsk and Luhansk. These oblasts were areas where Russian separatists had been fighting the Ukrainian government. Putin ordered Russian troops to the area, falsely claiming they were there to help keep the peace. In response, the United States, the United Kingdom, and the European Union, among other international powers, issued sanctions against Russian banks and oil and natural gas exports.

In the early morning of February 24, 2022, President Zelenskyy made an address to the Russian people from Ukraine's capital. He encouraged them to embrace peace and warned them that

Ukraine would defend itself against Russian invasion. At 6:00 a.m., President Putin declared that he was starting a "special military operation" in Ukraine.[4] Putin claimed that he was sending troops to Ukraine to demilitarize it and remove leaders he falsely claimed were neo-Nazis. He also claimed the invasion was a preemptive move of self-defense against the West. The Russian troops along the northern border and in Crimea invaded, and air raid sirens wailed as explosions occurred in Ukraine's eastern region.

On the first day of the invasion, Russian troops targeted Ukrainian military assets. Troops closed in around Kharkiv in the northeast and Odesa in the south. Russian troops also made progress toward the coastal city of Mariupol in southeast Ukraine. In response, Ukraine sent soldiers to defend these cities. Ukrainian civilians who stayed behind gathered military and medical supplies. Others took down street signs in their cities and towns in an effort to confuse Russian troops.

Despite having an army a fraction of the size of Russia's, Ukraine's resistance was fierce. Russia's first attempts to capture Kyiv and Mariupol were unsuccessful. While it withdrew troops, Russia

## DISPLACED UKRAINIANS

Through July 2022, around 12 million people had fled the fighting in Ukraine.[5] In just the first week of fighting, more than one million people had crossed Ukraine's western border, primarily into neighboring Poland.[6] Most of the refugees were women, children, and the elderly. Men aged 18 to 60 were required to stay in Ukraine and fight. At the same time, more than about 150,000 civilians have joined the volunteer army to defend it from Russian attack.[7]

struck Kyiv with long-range missiles. These attacks damaged military assets in Ukraine. But they also damaged apartment complexes, hospitals, and public transportation infrastructure. Civilians in Kyiv reported evidence of possible war crimes committed against Ukrainians. These included possible executions and torture. In Mariupol, satellite images showed that Russian attacks had damaged 90 percent of the city.[8] Images also found possible evidence of mass graves. Thousands of Ukrainian civilians were injured or killed in the attacks on Kyiv and Mariupol.

After its failure to capture Kyiv and Mariupol in March, Russia regrouped for an attack in the Donbas region of eastern Ukraine. The invasion began on April 9, 2022. In response to fighting in the Donbas, Ukrainian forces launched a counterattack in Kharkiv. This attack pushed Russian forces in the northeast back toward the Russian border. Meanwhile, Russian forces in Donbas clashed with Ukrainian forces. Russia renewed its efforts to retake the city of Mariupol. On May 16, Russia succeeded after surrounding the remaining Ukrainian forces who were defending the nearby Azovstal Iron and Steel Works plant. In June 2022, Russian forces continued to hold the city of Mariupol.

**Up to 9,000 people may be buried in the mass grave outside Mariupol, according to the Mariupol City Council.[9]**

By mid-May, experts estimated the war in Ukraine would last much longer than Russia had anticipated. Despite its larger military, Russian forces suffered significant losses in the first few

Russia's bombing of Ukraine resulted in the displacement and death of many Ukrainian civilians and soldiers.

### WESTERN UKRAINE'S RESPONSE TO WAR

Most of the fighting in the war in Ukraine has occurred in the eastern region of the country. However, Ukrainians in western cities and towns have been affected by the war too. Many eastern Ukrainians fled west when fighting broke out. Hundreds of thousands of refugees traveled to the western city of Lviv. Residents, churches, and schools in Lviv took in many of these refugees. Others took up arms and traveled to eastern Ukraine to fight.

months of the war. By some estimates, Russia had lost approximately 1,000 tanks, 350 pieces of artillery, and dozens of fighter planes.[10] In July 2022, up to 15,000 Russian soldiers had been killed in the conflict.[11] In Ukraine, more than 10,000 civilian and military deaths were reported at the end of June.[12]

Ukraine has maintained its independence despite aggression and occupation by multiple powers over the last few centuries, including Russia's large-scale invasion in February 2022. Ukrainians continue to celebrate their distinct culture, language, and national identity.

# ESSENTIAL **FACTS**

## OFFICIAL NAME: UKRAINE

### GEOGRAPHY

Area: 233,032 square miles (603,550 sq km)

Highest Elevation: Mount Hoverla at 6,762 feet (2,061 m)

Lowest Elevation: Black Sea at 0 feet (0 m)

### PEOPLE

Population: 43.5 million (2022 est.)

Most Populous City: Kyiv (2.8 million)

Ethnic Groups: Ukrainian, Russian, Tatar, Hutsul, Jewish

Religions: Christianity (Eastern Orthodoxy, Ukrainian Greek Catholicism, Roman Catholicism, Protestantism)

### GOVERNMENT

Type of Government: Semi-presidential republic

Capital: Kyiv

Head of State: President

Head of Government: Prime minister

Legislature: Unicameral, with the Verkhovna Rada

### ECONOMY

Currency: Hryvnia

Major Industries: Agriculture, coal, food processing, machinery and transport equipment

Natural Resources: Iron ore, coal, timber, natural gas, graphite, farmland

## NATIONAL SYMBOLS

National Anthem: “Shche ne vmerla Ukrainy” (“Ukraine Has Not Yet Perished”)

National Bird: Common nightingale

National Flower: Sunflower

# GLOSSARY

**ANNEX**
To take a part of land or territory, typically by force.

**DIALECT**
A regional variety of a language with distinct vocabulary, grammar, and accent.

**GENOCIDE**
Widespread, systematic acts of violence intended to destroy a national, ethnic, racial, or religious group.

**KHANATE**
An area governed by a leader called a khan.

**MONOPOLY**
Exclusive ownership of an entire industry or economic sector.

**NORTH ATLANTIC TREATY ORGANIZATION (NATO)**
A military alliance of North American and European nations.

**PRINCIPALITY**
A territory governed by a prince.

## QUAY
A human-made structure used as a landing place along a waterway.

## SANCTION
An action taken to punish a country or force it to follow international laws.

## SATIRIZE
To use irony, wit, and sarcasm to discredit a subject.

## SEPARATIST
A person who supports the independence of a region within a country.

## SOCIALIST
Having to do with socialism, a political and economic theory that advocates resources and property being shared equally among members of society.

## UNICAMERAL
Having a single legislative chamber.

# ADDITIONAL **RESOURCES**

## SELECTED BIBLIOGRAPHY


Di Duca, Marc, Greg Bloom, and Leonid Ragozin. *Ukraine*. Lonely Planet, 2018.

Stebelsky, Ihor, et al. "Ukraine." *Encyclopedia Britannica*, 2 Mar. 2022, britannica.com. Accessed 22 Mar. 2022.

Subtelny, Orest. *Ukraine: A History*. University of Toronto Press, 2009.

"Ukraine." *CIA World Factbook*, 15 Mar. 2022. cia.gov. Accessed 22 Mar. 2022.


## FURTHER READINGS


Britton, Tamara L. *War in Ukraine*. Abdo, 2022.

Edwards, Sue Bradford. *Russia*. Abdo, 2023.

Wheeler, Jill C. *Volodymyr Zelenskyy*. Abdo, 2022.


## ONLINE RESOURCES

To learn more about Ukraine, please visit **abdobooklinks.com** or scan this QR code. These links are routinely monitored and updated to provide the most current information available.

## MORE INFORMATION

For more information on this subject, contact or visit the following organizations:

**Embassy of Ukraine in the United States of America**
3350 M St. NW
Washington, DC 20007
usa.mfa.gov.ua/en
The Ukrainian embassy's website includes information about Ukraine and its relationship with the United States.

**National Museum of the Holodomor-Genocide**
Lavrska St., 3,
Kyiv, Ukraine 01015
holodomormuseum.org.ua/en
The National Museum of the Holodomor-Genocide educates people about the Holodomor genocide through exhibitions, film screenings, and educational projects.

**Ukrainian Institute of America**
2 East 79th St.
New York, NY 10075
ukrainianinstitute.org
The Ukrainian Institute of America is a nonprofit organization that promotes the art, literature, and music of Ukraine. It hosts art exhibits, concerts, and other events.

# SOURCE **NOTES**

## CHAPTER 1. MEMORIES OF UKRAINE

1. "Dnipro Population 2022." *World Population Review*, n.d., worldpopulationreview.com. Accessed 20 July 2022.
2. "Dnipro." *Eco Friendly Travels*, n.d., ecofriendlytravels.com. Accessed 20 July 2022.
3. "Affordable MBBS Tuition, Cheap to Live in: Why Students Study in Ukraine." *Study International*, 7 Mar. 2022, studyinternational.com. Accessed 20 July 2022.
4. Monica Mark. "Racism Is Another War Front for African Students Stuck in Ukraine." *Christian Science Monitor*, 4 Mar. 2022, csmonitor.com. Accessed 20 July 2022.
5. "Ukraine." *CIA World Factbook*, 15 July 2022, cia.gov. Accessed 20 July 2022.
6. "Men's Ranking." *FIFA*, 31 Mar. 2022, fifa.com. Accessed 20 July 2022.

## CHAPTER 2. GEOGRAPHY

1. "Ukraine Summary." *Encyclopedia Britannica*, britannica.com. n.d., Accessed 20 July 2022.
2. "Where is Ukraine in the World?" *World Population Review*, n.d., worldpopulationreview.com. Accessed 20 July 2022.
3. Orest Subtelny. *Ukraine: A History*. University of Toronto Press, 2000. 3.
4. Ihor Stebelsky, et al. "Ukraine." *Encyclopedia Britannica*, 17 June 2022, britannica.com. Accessed 20 July 2022.
5. Stebelsky et al., "Ukraine," *Encyclopedia Britannica*.
6. "Danube Delta." *Rewilding Europe*, n.d., rewildingeurope.com. Accessed 20 July 2022.
7. "Oleshky Sands National Nature Park." *Nature Fund Reserve of Ukraine*, n.d., wownature.in.ua. Accessed 20 July 2022.
8. Stebelsky et al., "Ukraine," *Encyclopedia Britannica*.
9. Stebelsky et al., "Ukraine," *Encyclopedia Britannica*.
10. "Crimean Peninsula." *Encyclopedia Britannica*, n.d., britannica.com. Accessed 20 July 2022.
11. Stebelsky et al., "Ukraine," *Encyclopedia Britannica*.
12. Stebelsky et al., "Ukraine," *Encyclopedia Britannica*.
13. Daria Shulzhenko. "Alarming River Pollution Endangers Health, Environment." *Kyiv Post*, 31 July 2021, kyivpost.com. Accessed 20 July 2022.

## CHAPTER 3. PLANTS AND ANIMALS

1. "Askaniya-Nova Biosphere Reserve, Ukraine." *UNESCO*, n.d., en.unesco.org. Accessed 20 July 2022.
2. "Biosphere Reserve Askania-Nova." *Discover Kherson*, n.d., en.discoverkherson.com.ua. Accessed 20 July 2022.
3. "Biosphere Reserve Askania-Nova," *Discover Kherson*.
4. "The Bison Men of Ukraine." *Radio Free Europe Radio Liberty*, 26 Apr. 2021, rferl.org. Accessed 20 July 2022.
5. Ihor Stebelsky, et al. "Ukraine." *Encyclopedia Britannica*, 17 June 2022, britannica.com. Accessed 20 July 2022.
6. "Secrets of the Black Sea: How Many Species Live in the Black Sea?" *Odessa Journal*, 9 Dec. 2020, odessa-journal.com. Accessed 20 July 2022.
7. "How Chernobyl Has Become an Unexpected Haven for Wildlife." *UN Environment Programme*, 16 Sep. 2020, unep.org. Accessed 20 July 2022.
8. John R. Platt. "20 Endangered Species at Risk in Ukraine." *Revelator*, 28 Feb. 2022, therevelator.org. Accessed 20 July 2022.

## CHAPTER 4. HISTORY

1. Orest Subtelny. *Ukraine: A History*. University of Toronto Press, 2000. 6.
2. Subtelny, *Ukraine: A History*, 33.
3. Subtelny, *Ukraine: A History*, 57.
4. "Holodomor." *University of Minnesota*, n.d., cla.umn.edu. Accessed 20 July 2022.
5. Ali Rogin and Morgan Till. "Ukraine's History and Its Centuries-Long Road to Independence." *PBS*, 8 Mar. 2022, pbs.org. Accessed 20 July 2022.
6. Ihor Stebelsky, et al. "Ukraine." *Encyclopedia Britannica*, 17 June 2022, britannica.com. Accessed 20 July 2022.
7. Stebelsky et al., "Ukraine," *Encyclopedia Britannica*.
8. Stebelsky et al., "Ukraine," *Encyclopedia Britannica*.
9. Stebelsky et al., "Ukraine," *Encyclopedia Britannica*.
10. John-Thor Dahlburg. "Ukraine Votes to Quit Soviet Union: Independence: More than 90% of Voters Approve Historic Break with Kremlin. The President-Elect Calls for Collective Command of the Country's Nuclear Arsenal." *Los Angeles Times*, 3 Dec. 1991, latimes.com. Accessed 21 July 2022.

# SOURCE **NOTES** CONTINUED


## CHAPTER 5. PEOPLE AND CULTURE

1. "Ukraine." *CIA World Factbook*, 15 July 2022, cia.gov. Accessed 20 July 2022.
2. "Ukraine," *CIA World Factbook*.
3. "Ukraine," *CIA World Factbook*.
4. "How Many Ukrainian Refugees Are There and Where Have They Gone?" *BBC News*, 4 July 2022, bbc.com. Accessed 21 July 2022.
5. "Ukraine," *CIA World Factbook*.
6. "Kharkiv." *Encyclopedia Britannica*, 14 May 2022, britannica.com. Accessed 20 July 2022.
7. Ihor Stebelsky, et al. "Ukraine." *Encyclopedia Britannica*, 17 June 2022, britannica.com. Accessed 20 July 2022.
8. "Ukraine Wages: Minimum and Average." *Take-profit.org*, n.d., take-profit.org. Accessed 20 July 2022.
9. "Ukraine to Fight Gender Inequality in Education, at Work and Home." *ReliefWeb*, 27 Jan. 2021, reliefweb.int. Accessed 20 July 2022.
10. Amie Ferris-Rotman. "Ukrainian Women Are Mobilizing beyond the Battlefield to Defend Their Country." *Time*, 22 Mar. 2022, time.com. Accessed 20 July 2022.
11. "Ukraine," *CIA World Factbook*.
12. A Martínez, Joanna Kakissis, Reena Advani, Lisa Weiner, and Avery Keatley. "The Russian-Ukrainian Orthodox Church Schism Continues to Anger Moscow." *NPR*, 10 Feb. 2022, npr.org. Accessed 20 July 2022.
13. "The Holocaust in Ukraine." *EHRI Online Course in Holocaust Studies*, n.d., training.ehri-project.eu. Accessed 20 July 2022.
14. Alex Reid. "Fighters Vitali and Wladimir Are the Klitschko Brothers Who Survived Chernobyl, Became Boxing World Champions and Are Now Fighting for Ukraine against Russia alongside Oleksandr Usyk and Vasyl Lomachenko." *talkSPORT*, 8 Mar. 2022, talksport.com. Accessed 20 July 2022.

## CHAPTER 6. POLITICS

1. Ihor Stebelsky, et al. "Ukraine." *Encyclopedia Britannica*, 17 June 2022, britannica.com. Accessed 20 July 2022.
2. Stuart Williams, Daphne Benoit, and Valerie Leroux. "Ukrainian Forces Vastly Outnumbered and Outgunned by Russia Despite West's Help." *Times of Israel*, 24 Feb. 2022, timesofisrael.com. Accessed 20 July 2022.

## CHAPTER 7. ECONOMICS

1. Willem Buiter. "Ukraine's Choice: Corruption or Growth." *Atlantic Council*, 19 June 2021, atlanticcouncil.org. Accessed 20 July 2022.

2. Buiter, "Ukraine's Choice: Corruption or Growth," *Atlantic Council*.

3. "Ukraine." *CIA World Factbook*, 15 July 2022, cia.gov. Accessed 20 July 2022.

4. "Ukraine," *CIA World Factbook*.

5. Agnieszka Maciejewska and Katarzyna Skrzypek. "Ukraine Agriculture Exports – What Is at Stake in the Light of Invasion?" *IHS Markit*, 7 Mar. 2022, ihsmarkit.com. Accessed 20 July 2022.

6. Maciejewska and Skrzypek, "Ukraine Agriculture Exports," *IHS Markit*.

7. "Ukraine," *CIA World Factbook*.

## CHAPTER 8. UKRAINE TODAY

1. "Ukraine." *Reuters*, 15 July 2022, graphics.reuters.com. Accessed 20 July 2022.

2. "Ukraine." *CIA World Factbook*, 15 July 2022, cia.gov. Accessed 20 July 2022.

3. Patrick Wintour. "Russia Has Amassed up to 190,000 Troops on Ukraine Borders, US Warns." *Guardian*, 18 Feb. 2022, theguardian.com. Accessed 20 July 2022.

4. Nicole Werbeck and Dustin Jones. "Another Possible Mass Grave with as Many as 9,000 Bodies Is Found near Mariupol." *NPR*, 22 Apr. 2022, npr.org. Accessed 20 July 2022.

5. "How Many Ukrainian Refugees Are There and Where Have They Gone?" *BBC News*, 4 July 2022, bbc.com. Accessed 20 July 2022.

6. "How Many Ukrainian Refugees Are There and Where Have They Gone?" *BBC News*.

7. Alfred Hackensberger. "Ukrainian Families Are Being Ripped Apart as Men Stay Behind to Fight the Russian Invasion." *Insider*, 3 Mar. 2022, businessinsider.com. Accessed 20 July 2022.

8. "Conflict in Ukraine." *Council on Foreign Relations*, 12 May 2022. cfr.org. Accessed 20 July 2022.

9. Paulina Villegas. "New Mass Grave Points to War Crimes in Mariupol, Ukrainian Officials Say." *Washington Post*, 21 Apr. 2022, washingtonpost.com. Accessed 20 July 2022.

10. Ryan Pickrell. "US Believes Russia Has So Far Lost Nearly 1,000 Tanks in Putin's War with Ukraine, Defense Official Says." *Business Insider*, 26 May 2022, businessinsider.com. Accessed 20 July 2022.

11. Mark Moore. "US, UK Intel Chiefs Estimate 15,000 Russian Troops Killed in Ukraine War." *New York Post*, 21 July 2022, nypost.com. Accessed 1 Aug. 2022.

12. Rob England, et al. "War in Ukraine: Can We Say How Many People Have Died?" *BBC News*, 1 July 2022, bbc.com. Accessed 20 July 2022.

# INDEX

# ABOUT THE **AUTHOR**

## A. R. CARSER

A. R. Carser is a freelance writer who lives in Minnesota. She enjoys learning and writing about the history and culture of Ukraine and other countries.